Ages 3+

WONDER MAGIC ALPHABET

Practice Workbook For Preschoolers

Vanishing Ink | Reusable in 15 minutes | Thick Paper

Includes penholder, gripper and refills

Wonder House

Note I:

Extra-thick paper, no curling, the product uses the groove design to constrain the user's writing habits, use the special faded stylus pen, the writing will disappear automatically after writing, the basic handwriting is gone, the front handwriting has disappeared, no need to wait, Reusable, environmentally friendly and energy efficient.

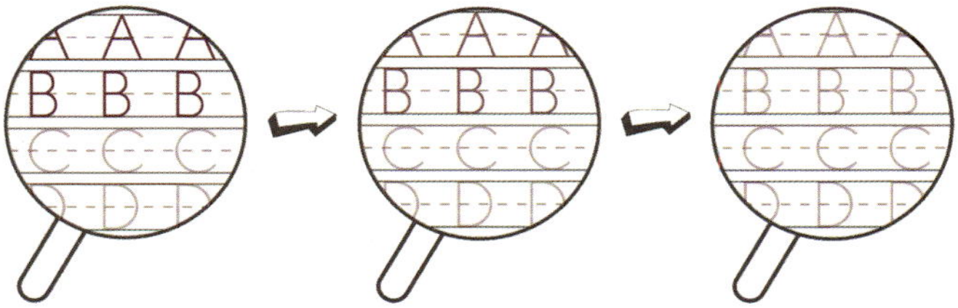

Note2:

This product is forbidden to wipe with force. Do not wipe with a damp cloth. Please keep it in a dry and ventilated place.

Note3:

1. Only use the special pen core for the product to write, the handwriting will disappear.
2. When the special pen core is in use, the ink may be clogged. Use the pen tip to lightly write several times on ordinary white paper, After the ink is smooth, then start the practice.
3. As the ink is specially processed, the handwriting will disappear after writing. Please do not use it for daily writing, record important information and sign documents, so as to avoid unnecessary losses to you.

Learn Alphabet

A a

apple

A A A A A A

a a a a a a a a a

B b

bee

B B B B B B

b b b b b b b b b

C c

cat

C C C C C C

c c c c c c c c c

D d

dog

D D D D D D

d d d d d d d d d

Fruits 

apple

tomato

strawberry

pineapple

cherry

watermelon

banana

lemon

Learn Alphabet

E e  eye

E E E E E E

e e e e e e e e e

F f  fish

F F F F F F

f f f f f f f f f

G g  goat

G G G G G G

g g g g g g g g g

H h  hand

H H H H H H

h h h h h h h h h

Stationery

pencil sharpener

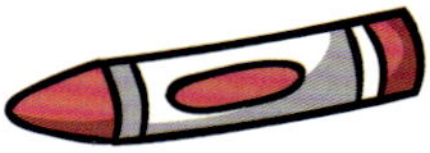

crayon

pencil case

book

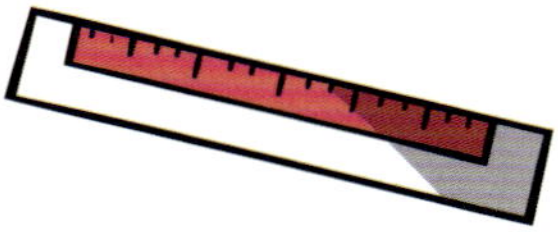

ruler

pen

eraser

schoolbag

Learn Alphabet

I i

ice cream

I I I I I I

i i i i i i i i i

J j

jelly

J J J J J J

j j j j j j j j j

K k

kite

K K K K K K

k k k k k k k k k

L l

lion

L L L L L L

l l l l l l l l l

Vehicles

train

car

aircraft

yacht

motorcycle

bicycle

bus

truck

Learn Alphabet

Mm

mango

M M M M M M

m m m m m m m m m

Nn

nose

N N N N N N

n n n n n n n n n

Oo

orange

O O O O O O

o o o o o o o o o

Pp

pen

P P P P P P

p p p p p p p p p

Animals

butterfly

elephant

bird

monkey

honeybee

lion

rooster

giraffe

Learn Alphabet

Q q

queen

Q Q Q Q Q Q

q q q q q q q q q

R r

rabbit

R R R R R R

r r r r r r r r r

S s

sun

S S S S S S

s s s s s s s s s

T t

tomato

T T T T T T

t t t t t t t t t

Sports

basketball

soccer

volleyball

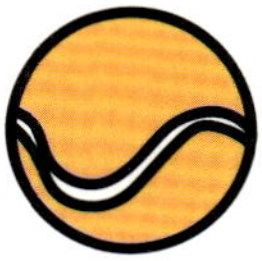

tennis

football

billiards

table tennis

tennis

Learn Alphabet

U u

ukelele

U U U U U U

u u u u u u u u u

V v

vulture

V V V V V V

v v v v v v v v v

W w

water

W W W W W W

w w w w w w w w w

X x

xiphias

X X X X X X

x x x x x x x x x

Food

pizza

hot dog

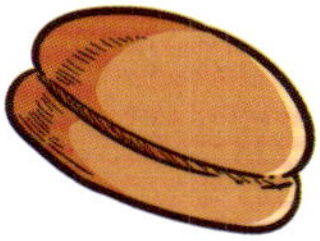

bread

hamburger

cake

ice cream

french fries

noodles

Learn Alphabet

Y y yolk

Y Y Y Y Y Y

y y y y y y y y y

Z z 0 zero

Z Z Z Z Z Z

z z z z z z z z z

Learn Alphabet

1 one

one one one one

2 two

two two two two

3 three

three three three

Body Parts

face

mouth

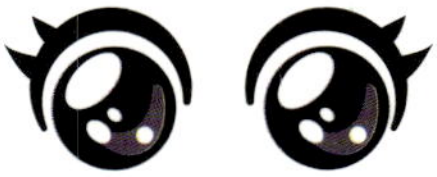

eye

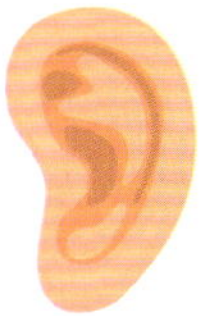

ear

teeth

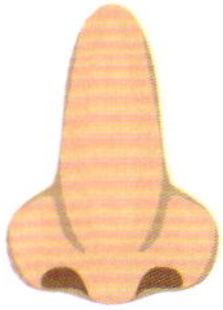

nose

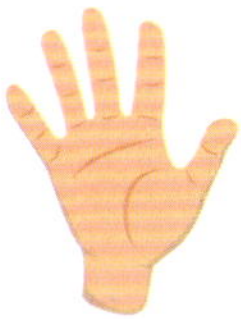

hand

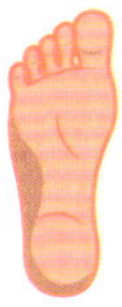

foot

Learn Alphabet

4 — four

four four four four

5 — five

five five five five

6 — six

six six six six

7 — seven

seven seven seven

8 — eight

eight eight eight

9 — nine

nine nine nine nine

10 — ten

ten ten ten ten

Vegetables

radish

mushroom

garlic

leek

chinese cabbage

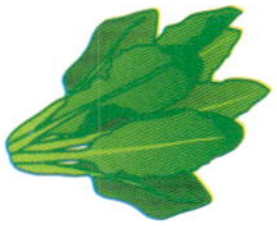

spinach

cucumber

eggplant

GOOD POSTURE

1.Both feet on the floor
2.Elbows off edge of desk
3.Sit back in the chair
4.Shoulders slightly forward
5.Proper desk height

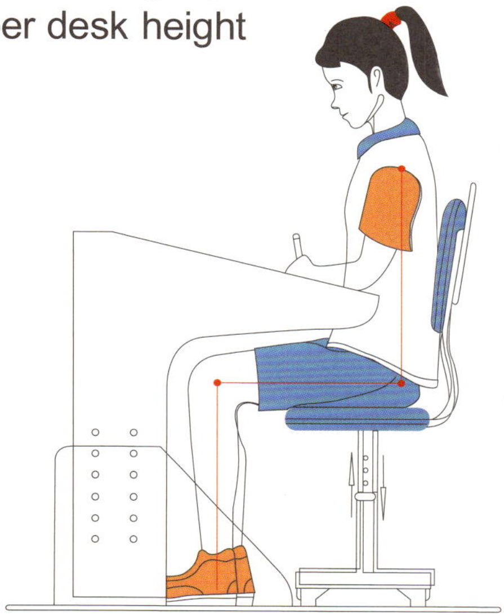

GOOD HANDWRITING

PAPER POSITION

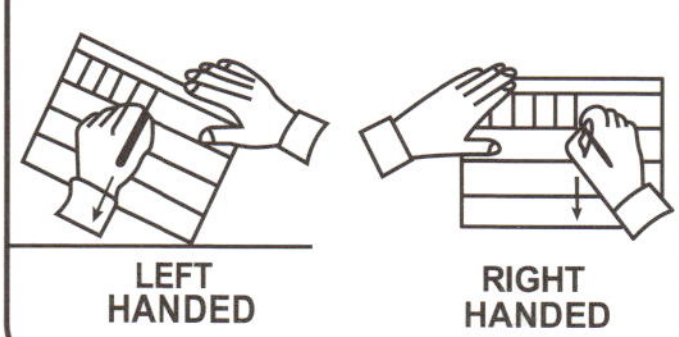

PENCIL POSITION

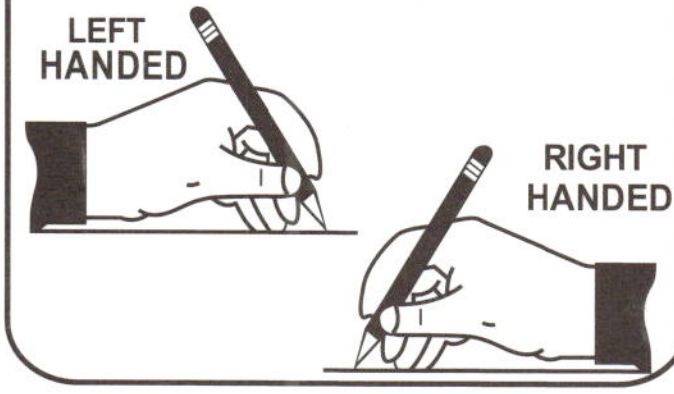

WONDER MAGIC ALPHABET

Practice Workbook For Preschoolers

Get ready to embark on a writing journey like no other! This interactive book for beginners with vanishing ink will inspire children to practice writing the alphabet repeatedly. The book allows beginners to enhance their handwriting skills by following the grooves to form perfect letters.

Let the interactive book guide you to write confidently and have fun!

Titles in the series

Wonder House

Wonder House Books is an imprint of Prakash Books

UK £ 1.99 CAN $ 4.99 US $ 2.99

ISBN: 978-93-6214-595-6

9 789362 145956

Wonder House

MRP

www.wonderhousebooks.com • 00005900

wonderhousebooks wonderhousebooks wonderhousebook